GREAT MOVIE Instrumental Solos

Play-Along Tracks with Full Performance Recordings!

TITLE	BOOK Page No.	CD TRACK DEMO	PLAY-ALONG
Tuning Note (B♭ Concert)		1	
Battle of the Heroes *Star Wars®: Episode III Revenge of the Sith*	2	2	3
Double Trouble *Harry Potter and the Prisoner of Azkaban*	4	4	5
Star Wars (Main Title) *Star Wars®: Episode III Revenge of the Sith*	5	6	7
Superman Theme *Superman Returns*	6	8	9
Raiders March *Raiders of the Lost Ark*	8	10	11
Hogwarts' Hymn *Harry Potter and the Goblet of Fire*™	10	12	13
Wonka's Welcome Song *Charlie & The Chocolate Factory*	11	14	15
The Imperial March *Star Wars®: Episode II Attack of the Clones*	12	16	17
The Notebook (Main Title) *The Notebook*	13	18	19
Into the West *The Lord of the Rings: The Return of the King*	14	20	21

© 2006 Alfred Publishing Co., Inc.
All Rights Reserved

Any duplication, adaptation or arrangement of the compositions contained in this collection requires the written consent of the Publisher. No part of this book may be photocopied or reproduced in any way without permission. Unauthorized uses are an infringement of the U.S. Copyright Act and are punishable by law.

DEMO 4 PLAY ALONG 5

DOUBLE TROUBLE

Music by
JOHN WILLIAMS

Medieval in spirit (♩ = 92)

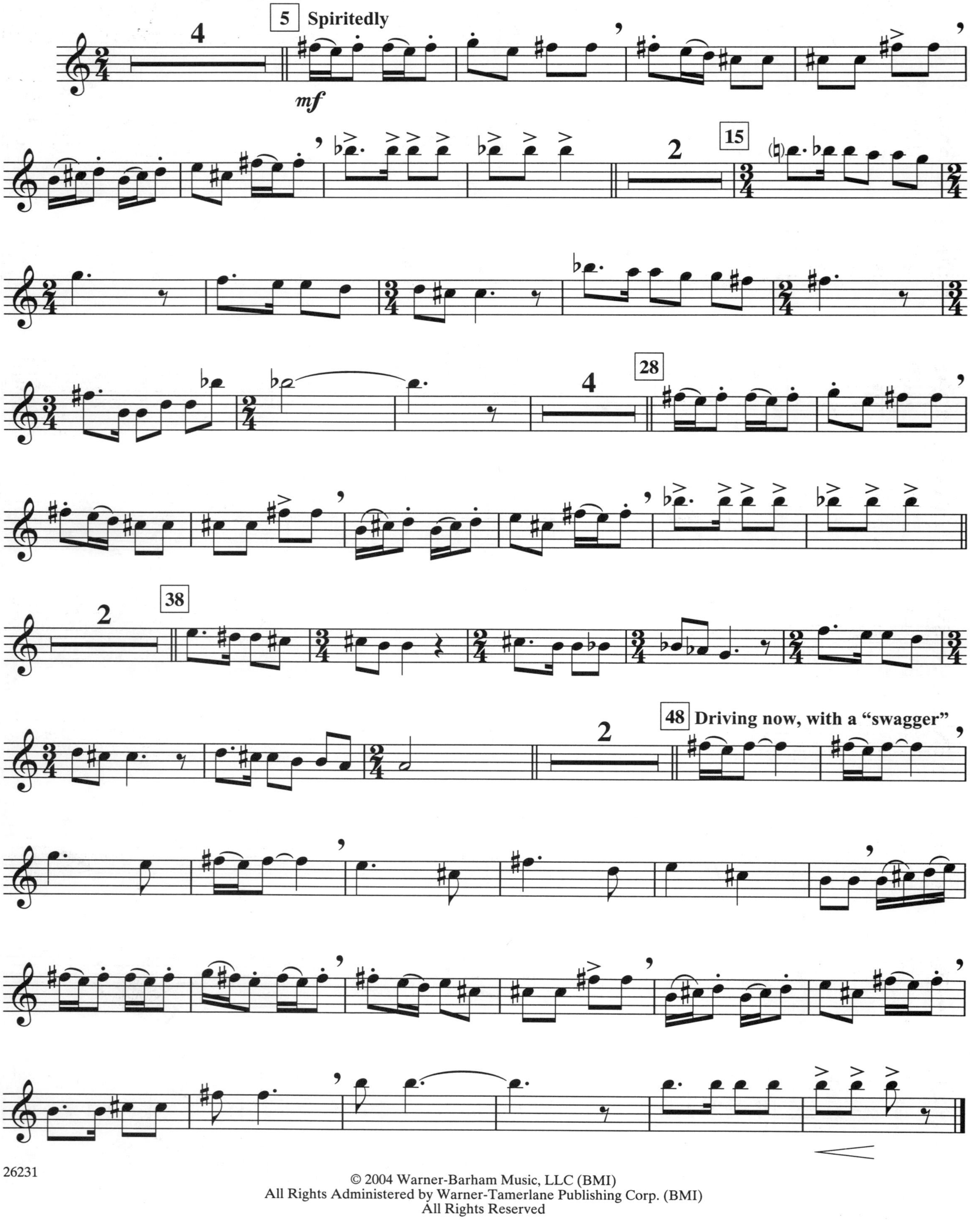

© 2004 Warner-Barham Music, LLC (BMI)
All Rights Administered by Warner-Tamerlane Publishing Corp. (BMI)
All Rights Reserved

SUPERMAN THEME

Music by
JOHN WILLIAMS

RAIDERS MARCH

Music by
JOHN WILLIAMS

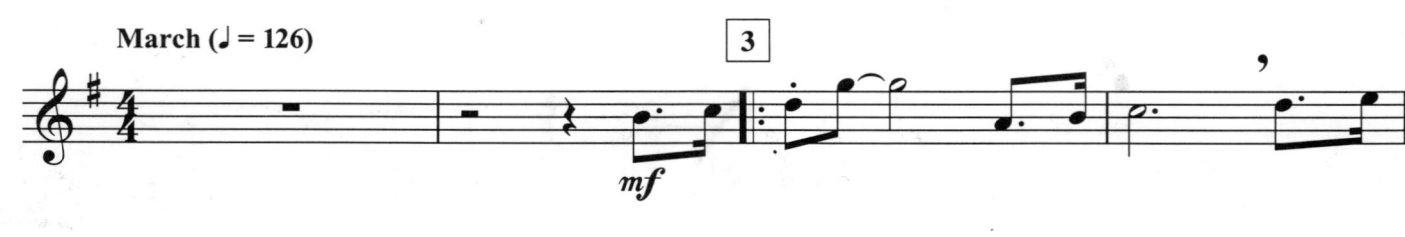

© 1981 BANTHA MUSIC and ENSIGN MUSIC CORPORATION
All Rights for the World Controlled and Administered by ENSIGN MUSIC CORPORATION
All Rights Reserved   Used by Permission

HOGWARTS' HYMN

By PATRICK DOYLE

WONKA'S WELCOME SONG

Music by DANNY ELFMAN
Lyrics by JOHN AUGUST and DANNY ELFMAN

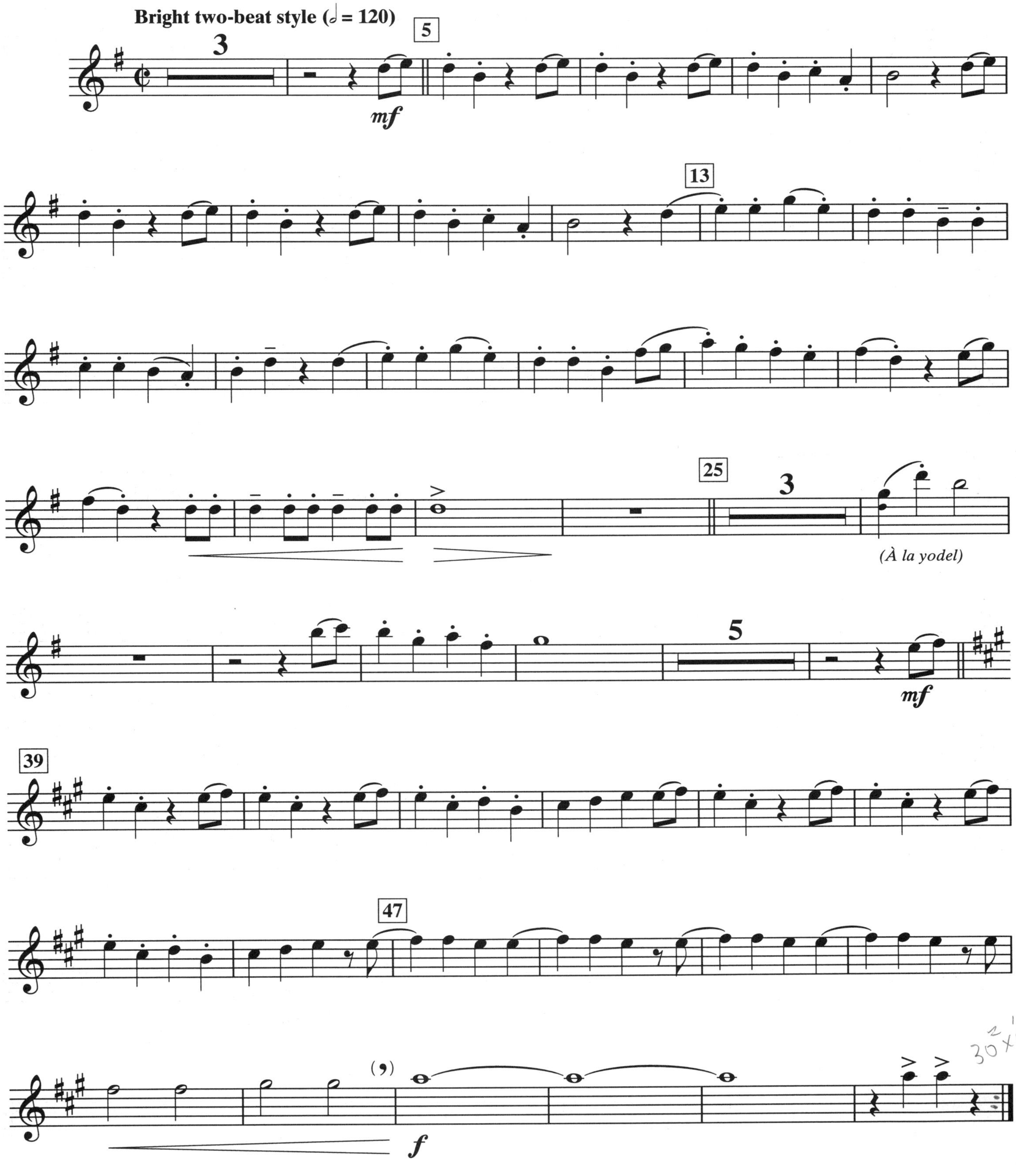

THE IMPERIAL MARCH
(Darth Vader's Theme)

Music by **JOHN WILLIAMS**

INTO THE WEST

Words and Music by
HOWARD SHORE, FRAN WALSH,
ANNIE LENNOX

Into the West - 2 - 1
26231

© MMIII New Line Tunes (ASCAP)/BMG Songs Inc. (ASCAP) obo La Lennoxa Limited/
BMG Music Publishing Ltd./South Fifth Avenue Publishing (ASCAP)
All Rights for New Line Tunes Administered by WB Music Corp. (ASCAP)
All Rights Reserved

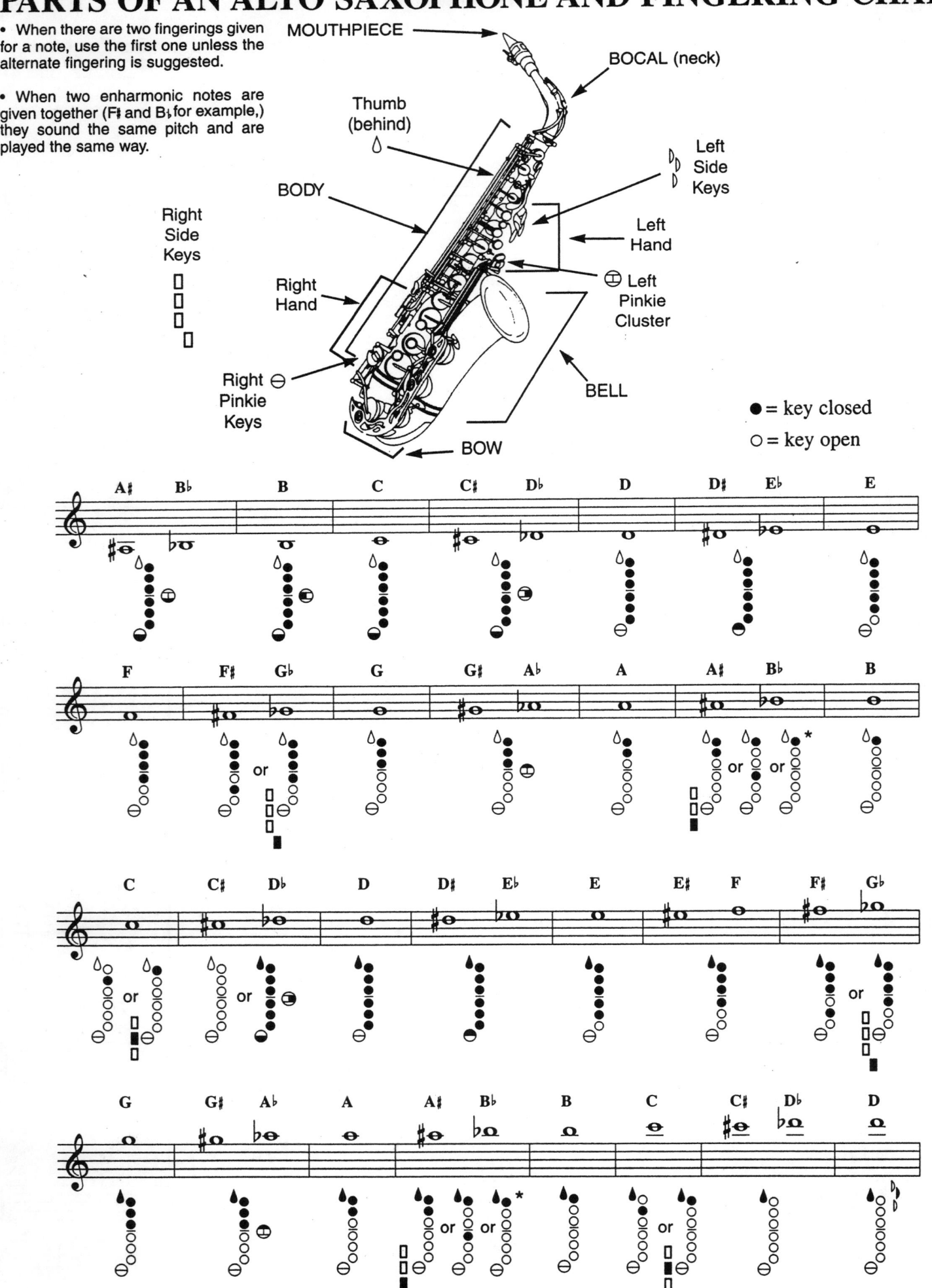